OGYGIA

Lisa Summers

FMRL

Petaluma, California

Ogygia

© 2014 by Lisa Summers
All rights reserved.

ISBN: 978-0-9671001-6-6

FMRL
HQ | 40 Fourth Street No. 111 | Petaluma, CA 94952
fmrl.com | info@fmrl.com | 707-340-3675

Daedalus Howell, Publisher
Scott Summers, Designer

Printed in the United States of America

Follow Lisa Summers on Twitter @the_bananafish

OGYGIA

Lisa Summers

FMRL
Petaluma, California

contents

Ogygia 1

Split Custody 4

Jenny Greenteeth 6

Judecca's Broom Closet 8

Apple Dolls 11

Boogie Man 14

After Entelechy, The Real 15

Noonday Devil 16

Dead End Street 19

Wondrous Cauldrons 23

Assorted Chocolates 24

Pixie of the Serengeti 27

A Brief History of Echoes 29

A Brief History of Bridges and Tunnels 32

A Brief History of Roots 37

A Fauna of Mirrors 40

The Kermit Kingdom 44

Pravda – a Found Poem 48

For #Camus on His 100th Birthday 52

Eulogy for Sycorax 56

Half Savage and Free 60

The Expedition 63

The Strait of Messina 67

The Visitors 69

Kabocha 75

For Wendy 79

Open Letter to Mammon 81

Mylar Sirens 85

For my mother
Marsha Susan Parker (1945-2014)

"The blackness of the night possessed water, air, and beach. It was the darkness of an older world, before Man. There was no sound but the all-enveloping, primeval sounds of wind blowing over water and sand, and of waves crashing on the beach. There was no other visible life – just one small crab near the sea."
—Rachel Carson, *The Edge of the Sea*

"For some time there was a widely held notion (zealously fostered by the daily press) to the effect that the 'thinking ocean' of Solaris was a gigantic brain, prodigiously well-developed and several million years in advance of our own civilization, a sort of 'cosmic yogi', a sage, a symbol of omniscience, which had long ago understood the vanity of all action and for this reason had retreated into an unbreakable silence."
—Stanisław Lem, *Solaris*

"Goddess of song, teach me the story of a hero."
—Homer

Ogygia

On Ogygian shores Calypso lived
with two daughters, wild and fair,
each with eyes of pale moonstone
and hellebore strewn in their hair;
by day they bathed in sylvan pools
beneath the winding stair.

Ogygia, shimmering prison,
past the shrouded mist yet lies
three thousand leagues from here or more
as the Wandering Albatross flies;
for the man now long since departed
O'er the thundering waves she cries.

> *The sea, the sea, the roaring sea*
> *Delivered me he who was drowned!*
> *The man who was king and pulpit drunk*
> *wore a tangle of kelp for a crown!*

Ogygia, lost in the bounding main
under sepia lighted brume,
the wine-dark sky makes cruel silhouettes
on his weeping heart weeping for home.
Into her arms, her warm oubliette,
(always pulpit drunk he went)
of drinking her secret perfume.

Oh, such wroth experiments!
From dead meaning concrete towers;
those green light electric cigarettes
grow indigo harmony flowers.
No butts to junk his monuments
for seven long years of hours.

> *The sea, the sea, the roaring sea*
> *Delivered me he who was drowned!*
> *The man who was king and pulpit drunk*
> *wore a tangle of kelp for a crown!*

Fair Nausithous, wild Nausinous –
their miasma, a jasminey breeze;
it whips up the fever, it blisters the skin,
it coughs in the rustling leaves;
it buries the bones and steals the last breath
of dark indigo harmonies.

Ogygia, the watchers spy the white sails
billowing far upon the reach;
the moon-calf shakes the monkey pods,
slink prowling on the beach.
He is going home tonight
in swift ships beyond the reach.

> *The sea, the sea, the roaring sea*
> *Delivered me he who was drowned!*
> *The man who was king and pulpit drunk*
> *wore a tangle of kelp for a crown!*

The Seabees make poison honey
that drips in bomb drops from the comb;
blown bits of Ogygia's stone coral skirts
churn in irradiant foam;
the sand is aglow with the half-light
of eyes set in pale moonstone.

Return, return, my flotsam king!
Through the ages she scours the shore.
Now he comes by air in a squadron of bees –
She is post detonation
a nuclear sensation –
Have you seen her electric hair?

Calypso, Queen Bikini Atomic
is the child of a Titan-Atlas affair.

> *The sea, the sea, the roaring sea*
> *Delivered me he who was drowned!*
> *The man who was king and pulpit drunk*
> *wore a tangle of kelp for a crown!*
>
> *Now I with my daughters*
> *we search the clear waters*
> *for we who were lost and then found.*

Split Custody

In the dark hollows of winter nights
I walk the west side blocks of Broadway
where a few old mansions still stand –
one, a life insurance office, another a pet clinic.

There is a certain stretch of sidewalk
where new streetlights cast a sickly light,
where the pavement buckles from
the surface roots of the London Planetrees.

The effect is not entirely unpleasant;
one imagines the grand boulevards, the parks
of an old European city - *La Belle Époque*
under an alee of shadows, half lit by a gaslight glow.

I walk here often as relief from the blight
of parking lots, the housing tracts,
the portables of the elementary school
deposited by some great flood.

By the end of the block our stage set ends
at a gateway of a sort: a 76 station,
a Quick Stop, a print shop, a used car lot
bindweed in the asphalt, soda cups in the gutter.

Two little boys play in the entrance
of the Villa Allegra courtyard
where their mother smokes in the shadows
blowing smoke rings in the night fog.

At the curb, tidily stacked, are some overnight things:

> two pairs of tattered canvas sneakers
> two worn backpacks, the zipper broken on one
> a comfort blanket, rolled and strapped,
> still bearing last summer's burrs –
> a soiled stuffed rabbit
> a sippie cup
> two tin Batman lunch boxes.

These things, mute familiars of children,
stand vigil in the late hours.

The little boys give chase –
hero, villain, hero, villain;
the mother stands silently in the bone chilling air.

They could be waiting
for the rolling in of tanks
for the Boogie Man
for the Chitty Chitty child catcher
for an asteroid on course for Earth
for an Axis of Evil air strike
for Gotham to fall
for Godzilla to rise
for Mothra to descend.

When she thinks of her ex,
in the shadows she thinks,
They might as well be.

Jenny Greenteeth

From the misty heather moorland
Down the green, moss matted stair,
Walks the girl in heathen rags
With bluebells in her hair;
In her hand, the deadly nightshade
Blossoms from the glade.
She's come by way of Doxey Pond
By the bulrush, reed and frond,
Where moths and blow wives flutter
O'er blooms of witch's butter,
Before the night pulls tight its shutters
At the coming of the dawn.

She sings *trill* and *la* and *tralla-dee*!
Under shadows of the batches;
By stunted oak and withered beech
On wind wild nights she watches
For the nightjar in the trees
To sing his somber melodies.
She's come by way of Doxey Pond
By the bulrush, reed and frond,
Where milk-white moonbeams shatter
On the black and silent water
As the night pulls tight its shutters
Before the coming of the dawn.

In the peat dark waters whisper
The phantoms of the deeps
Of an age old coppiced wood
Where the ancient Mere Witch sleeps
Her stony ancient sleep.
Still the peat dark waters seep
Behind the crumbling cottage walls
Draped with pennywort and fern –
In the East a darkness falls
where the elfin bonfires burn.

By the Erl King's ancient throne
Made of silversand and stone,
They dance beneath the starless skies
And cry: "Awake, Old Jenny Greenteeth
From your deep and troubled sleep!"
Then away the Mere Witch flies!
Still, the girl in heathen rags
With faded blue-bells in her hair
Climbs the green moss-matted stair.

She goes her way by Doxey Pond
By the bulrush, reed and frond
When the flames are all but gone
No moths and blow wives flutter
For the night's locked tight its shutters
To stop the coming of the dawn.

*inspired by Christopher Somerville's *Britain and Ireland's Best Wild Places*

Judecca's Broom Closet

In Dante's Ninth and final Circle
there exists a hidden chamber where those
sinners against the greatest of all Benefactors,
that warm bosom of man known as Motherhood,
tremble in the icy darkness,
wide-eyed insomniacs who snored, and thus
slept indifferently through life.

Nobody speaks of this concealed room
known amongst the guards as Judecca's Broom Closet.

It isn't marked on any medieval map or chart
no stairs lead down to it
no doors lead out of it
it lies at the very center of a pathless void
a great din surrounds it, drowning
the gently sounding stream,
narrow watershed of the stars.

Even the purest of souls recoil, retreat
cower at the roar of wailing infants
broadcast, night and day, through speaking trumpets
hidden deep in the gaping mouths of Dis
that long ago spat out their Brutus
their Cassius, their Judas.

The emperor of the despondent kingdom,
towering mid-chest from his frozen pond,
has weathered, stiffened in limb and vigor;
yet, the women who guard Inferno's last stop,
ever resourceful, have found various new uses
for his rigid batwings –

> a coat tree
> a rack for drying towels
> and beating rugs
> for hanging hammocks
> cloth for sails and linens
> bone for hoop skirts
> parasols
> shower curtains

In life, these sinners bred this somnambulistic
army of wives, lovers, young mothers;
they kept them awake at all hours of the night
with their infernal raucous
their pig snorts, their sawing of logs
the diesel truck brakes
their low flying jets
their symphonies of pink noise.

These men never heard the babies crying.
They never heard the mice scamper or
the windows shatter.
Here is always night, but the weary never rest.

Cursed until the Rapture to stay awake until it comes
icy water is thrown upon
the snoring dosers and nodders offer
boiling pitch upon the cat napper, the hay-hitter
the telephone is off the hook
the coffee is always weak
the toast is cold, the eggs are raw
the game is over
the beer is flat
the charcoal is wet
the itch cannot be scratched.

Such a small price, say the women,
for interrupting so many lifetimes of dreams.

Apple Dolls

In the fruiting seasons
of their youth
they were crisp and firm
green and tart, juicy
and some might say *tempting*

They had once splashed
in the whitewash
of a blue Pacific,
their blonde hair
catching the wind
like scarves spun of sunlight

They had once gathered
by the river's edge
swimming in the emerald pools
while peevish boys
spied, hidden in the trees
one hand on a fishing pole
the other fumbling in a pocket

These suburban sirens,
these riverine selkies and
half-shelled Venuses,
these copper toned goddesses
basked in the last rays
of a summer sun,
having traded their voices
for the scaled tail of a fish

Now they sit poolside –
with spotted hands they
stir the ice cubes
melting in the gin

Someone's son is dating her hair dresser
another has new granite countertops
one has a new jawline

They don't dare go near the water
where the Lady of the Lake
holds her hand mirror to the gazers,
where Narcissus has dropped
all his frail white petals in the mud

Years later, someone notices that
a member of the party has gone missing,
gone quite literally, to seed
Nobody speaks of Her

Surely She's cracked –
planting her pockets of beans,
sunflowers and buckwheat,
bush lupines and poppies!

She wears the crow's feet about her eyes
a shaggy grey braid falls down her spine
full of burrs and foxtails

She buries acorns in the earth's hard crust
and offers libations
to the small hole in the ground
once covered by an inland sea

The towhee is in her kitchen
a fox nurses cubs below the porch
the hornets have chewed through
the walls of her shingled shack,
odd things sprout at her feet,
on her face a sort of lichen creeps

When a crack in the field appears one day
She finds the remains of an ancient shell
the wind still whispering in its chambers
guiding her to the distant mirage
of a sea shimmering
now returning to the plain

The others, still haunted by starlit encounters
with boys in the sultry heat,
still wading in the sapphire pools
where their reflections
told them Time was a
a bargain to strike –
They are the Apple Dolls

Poor wretches, says the One
Time makes such mockeries of maidenhood –
they have not a single seed saved
in their pockets left to offer.

Boogie Man

Of the thousands who fled the heat wave
simmering over the hills and valleys,
only a few brave the icy water
of the grey Pacific at Stinson Beach.

One, a weekend warrior type,
stuffed like a pepper in black neoprene,
rides a boogie board in on frothy foam
arriving on waves from places unknown.

On his face is a look of great surprise
and a suspicious joy as if he might
be asked to stop all this shameless exuberance
by a lifeguard or park ranger.

After his first failed attempt
to paddle out past the incoming set,
he rolls in, tangled up in the bull kelp
before hundreds of amused onlookers.

He laughs, throws up his arms in surrender
when the waves topples him, never minding
the children pointing as he, undaunted, boogies forth
and his wife looks worriedly away.

After Entelechy, The Real

Haven't you seen them? They were
asparagus green, such envious
wine cellar queens of the foothills
pills in their purses, one hand on the wheel.
Still, we endured; we penny saved
our azure dreams, our vital dunes,
scratching in the asphalt fields.

Ultrasound pictures, unborn empire builders
of pluripotent America:
You've no pity for the weak,
for your mother the flight risk,
for your father, the persevering chump,
for indeterminate democracies or
small disturbances in the atmosphere.

Stay a while. Try the silver aerosol!
Write 'Freedom Was Here!' on the concrete
walls of the headland bunker;
hug a sneering hipster on the train,
do something chivalric: stroll down Market
but don't feed the vagrants at City Hall
your cartons of curdled strawberry milk –
We're not pigeons, after all.

Noonday Devil

When you meet the Noonday Devil,
that spat shod snake of a spermologer,
that worm-tongued snoutfair,
you will know him by his oiled hair
his asphodelos crown
a rainforest emerald on his fingers
the bone dice clicking in his palm.

He wears a suit of camel hair.
The ruby-lipped girls
are always at his side.
He smiles a crooked smile,
chews gum of myrrh and mint
to mask his breath of lies.

He will find you sitting in the driver's seat
in your moment of despai,
stuck in a stagnant Nile of cars
flowing a sluggish inch an hour.

He will find you when your feeling
of complacency overwhelms you,
before the sublime terror of a new overpass
or the metal bones of a new shopping mall
or the steaming ground of clear-cut forest
where, looming in the acrid haze,
the monolithic mega-dam
pins you in its gaze.

Your mocha latte grows cold in the cup holder.
What are they screaming on the radio?

This Noonday Devil will make you an offer.
His servants will bring sugar water cakes
and iced tea spiked with absolution
to your car window on the highway.

He will ridicule what remains of
your Arcadian dreams,
trading them like cards
for a few thousand square feet
of floors made from the hardest woods,
a verdant patch of lawn,
a Technicolor future for your children,
a private box at Lucretia's playhouse.

You, in your moment of despair,
when your fear of complacency,
your helplessness in the face of seven billion
faceless pins on a spinning pincushion –
you may choose a troubled sleep
on velvet pillows over this waking hell.

In the fearful hours of the night
when the alley cats fight
and the sirens scream
when the late night t.v. pastors
and informercial preachers cull your dreams
when the trash cans
explode with the echoes

of far away city streets –
The Noonday Devil
will sing you softly back to sleep
with hymns he learned as a child.

He will take you in his wingéd chariot
to his Kingdom of Commerce.
You will be his Queen -
the Queen of all Cannibals.

One day you find yourself
in the passenger seat of a royal coach
with a retinue and velvet pillows,
staring up at the flag waving proudly
on the bridge of suicides
and you will awaken with
the Noonday Devil at your side.

You see it all plainly now.
The streets of his kingdom
are paved with bees.
The children weave his robes
on looms in the eternal night.

But what he doesn't know,
whisper the servant girls with ruby lips,
is the women are building an army
of wax dolls in his likeness,
and the dead will offer their pins.

Dead End Street

On a street in an old mill town
there live twenty six poets
in houses made of words.

The first, owner of the Greek Revival -
the Formalist - lives alone with his books;
stacked in columns, aligned in perfect rows
of equal heights; most are damaged by rain
falling through the holes in the old shake roof.

But just last year
        the Confessionals
had their house condemned.
        Now they roam the empty halls
listening to echoes and
        putting out their cigarettes
in the garden fountain
        while they bore each other
to stone with their lonely
        subjects.

Around the same time the Beats bought the dump next
door, a fixer upper if they had a dime; a hookah pipe
on the card table for the catepillar cat and metal folding
chairs for all the angel headed hipsters from the cold-
water flats.

When walking by,
one must avert the eyes

and ears from the waving
of Ginsberg's flaccid organ,
his Howling lips.
Ferlinghetti is still
constantly risking
absurdity and they
wonder why
there are so few women
in this pigsty of a
tent city.

    The Imagists...
what to make of this house –
a Funhouse of Mirrors
with shifting walls
concealed staircases;
the doors melt
in the doorjambs,
the glaciers knock in
the kitchen cupboards,
a bowl of pears that hold
summer in their purple hearts.

    The Haiku Poets
    walk up the mountain at dawn
    past the Tenements

        They cast blue shadows
        at the north end of the street
        when the banks foreclosed

At last they join the Romantics,
heavy hearted and consumptive,
gathered on steep and lofty cliffs
beyond the Hermit's Cave
looking down upon the ruined earth,
all of its defiled Edens
praying to indifferent gods
and pagan deities painted on urns
as the beautiful souls float by
like smoke rings in the breeze
they who have forsaken
the very idea of going home.

At the edge of a wood sits a cottage
made of moss-covered stone,
last house on the left –
The House of the Moths.
Beyond the wrought iron gate
form and sound burble,
retreat into nothing.

Home to alter boys and waifs
slaves and concubines
housewives and pill poppers
border jumpers, squatters
tree huggers, rub dubbers
fairy Dairy Queens
depressives and junkies,

The Man from Nantucket
standing on a bucket
singing sea shanties and
juke box singles –

These are the Outsiders,
their voices softer than a murmur,
fluttering in the darkness, spinning silk,
yet no longer waiting for someone to turn
the key rusting in the lock.

Wondrous Cauldrons

Iron cauldrons boil the tusks
inside deep indigo night
the rattling leaves, the jungle heat
the stench of gunsmoke
and rancid meat
    The matriarch waits
    in the shadows for Nganga woman
    to conjure her daughters
    her sons, her sisters
    from the boiling waters
        A Chinaman squats by the fire
        carving ivory Buddha Man,
        nearby sits the Wall Street wife
        the neighborhood thugs
        bush pilots and snipers;
        the spirit girl in the trees tells a secret:
            an elephant never forgets
            the poacher's face
            nor her tiny voice who, in
            hoarse whispers, told the baboons
            to pour sugar in the gas tanks,
            drop dead rats in the wells
                Soon this orphan will join the others,
                they will ride upon the high shoulders
                of three million childless mothers;
                the ivory will bleed sundown rivers
                into the streets of Hong Kong –
                watering hole of hungry ghosts.

Assorted Chocolates

Each piece in the Colonial Assortment
is an uncharted island
in the Tropics of Sample,
a sweet shop case of
brown paper lily pads
from which you hop
flavor to flavor.

Salted Almond Caramels
are an island honeymoon,
South Pacific whitewash at your toes
an endless horizon of
Ganache Bliss – beyond, the
the shadow of distant islands
under Scotchmallow skies.

Raspberry Creams
are the velvety blonde hairs
on your lover's suntanned neck;
Butterscotch lollies,
the sensation on your tongue
of his still warm skin and
and a midnight swim
with Praline Turtles.

Dark Bordeaux is a bloody ritual
a dithyramb (the jungle nocturn)
the cannibal's matrimonial
the last dance of the native virgins
before the slave traders' run.

Vanilla Walnut Fudge is daybreak,
a well-deserved stomach ache.
And for gluttonous mistakes,
Peanut Butter Patties
take the cake.

Bridge Mix has an aftertaste like
giardia at summer camp;
it makes you shiver and wretch,
cold sweats in your mummy bag.

Ginger Clusters are gymnasium-spiced,
with notes of basketball socks, jock straps
your square dancing partner's
clammy hands and sideways glances.

Mint Meltaways are nice like
Greenland's shrinking ice.
Polar Bears Paws (nuts and
nougat in white chocolate,
oft called Bon Bons of Extinction)
are as delicious to Tamora
as Chiron and Demetrius.

Inside the Coconut Creme,
the texture of childhood
goes stale, killing you softly
abandoning you to the long years
of Brittles and Toffees.

Nuts and Chews are a plate of
oily noodle kugel on the table
stuffy sitting rooms of uncles
talking politics and cataracts
at the party where you chew
in closet with the coats
hoarding chocolates from your sister
every minute growing sicker.

The last Rum Nougat, half-eaten
is the poison bait, stinking like
an Old Colonial's sour breath
too close to your mouth,
inhaling when he whispered,
laid a hand on your skinny thigh,
then sent the Colonial Assortment
to your father as a gift,
in exchange for your sickly silence.

Pixie of the Serengeti

In spite of all the hardship and destitution sagas –
covered wagons with busted wheels, Indian wars
short grass prairies and dried up wells –
most Panhandle stories involve beer and broken cars.

Standing two inches shy of five feet,
my grandmother Pixie wore horned-rim glasses,
kept her hair trimmed just over her ears
like it had been cut by fairies in a storm.

Once, half-way home from Dumas
just ninety south of nowhere
Grampa Grove's beloved lemon yellow
Chevy Impala overheated and stalled,
stranding us on the iron skillet highway.

There we were – the vanishing asphalt mirages,
my sister and I stuck like glue to the beige vinyl,
panting cows behind barbed wire
the Texan sky raining grasshoppers,
with Pixie and a six-pack of Coors tall cans.

After an hour or so of waiting for help to arrive,
Pixie cracked a warm one:
>> *Cain't hurt!*

The whole time I'm thinking about serial killers,
cuz I'd read about the Town That Dreaded Sundown,
or an eighteen-wheeler with bad brakes
or maybe never getting back to the ranch, ever.

Had I known what courage it had taken to
weather the dust storms, with everything dying,
and that punishing Great Plains sun blotted out,
how it covered their blankets, filled their mouths –

I might have worried less about
one old Impala that couldn't run.

1. A Brief History of Echoes

Womanhood had come to her in a war zone,
after the time when the dune grasses
and chaparral had been cleared and scorched,
the wetlands drained and the creeks diverted
around the undulated greens, all making way
for the terracotta villas – those uncanny colonies
sprawling as far as the eye could see and beyond

She left the sea for a high hilltop cave and sang
into the void, listening for the song of hydrogen

For many years, she heard only voices of machines
the blood-curdling anthems of tyrants and
the shrieking of their terracotta villa wives who,
after French manicures and Thai massages
juiced beets with burdock roots,
after holding a benefit to benefit
the last polar bears and running caribou, now
needing new homes in the lower forty-eight
because pipelines need straight lines–
she heard the sound of Nothing for the first time

Meanwhile, on far-off Io, interstellar sirens
heard her gentle song echoing in their
Jovian conk shells, and they pulled the anchor of
their iron rock, and set a course for the small sapphire
of Anthemoessa, breaking the sound waves with their
cold frequencies, following a lonely current

Circe, fierce captain on the bridge, piloted
the great rock across the oceans of eternal night;
the ship broke the ice fields of Saturn's rings
with its mighty iron hulls, sailed fearlessly to Earth
into the eye of a perfect storm of unlistening

Over time, the iron oxide dust on her plastic
skin began to rearrange itself, and so
the ambient terracotta villa Muzak piped in
through holes in the houses of the Lotus Eaters
became both Requiem and Prelude,
inaudible to all except her, there and alone,
listening from her hilltop cave to the silent void
with nothing but a small human heart

She, shopworn oracle, foresaw that the next age
would begin with chimes in the driftwood eaves
with the shape of laughter in the darkness
with the hushabye of pine needles on a granite peak,
with the ring of a monk's singing bowl washed up with
the plastic debris of the evening tide

It would begin with the wind whistling through
the wasted miles of organ pipes laid in the oily tundra
where the metal had rotted, and the wind,
blowing around the bones of the polar bears
and the caribou and of the cannibal men
whispered of changes not yet known

Humming softly to this ancient song,
suddenly recalled in her hilltop cave,
the woman made a small fire - a beacon
for Our Ladies of the Iron Rock
who were so weary from their journey.

2. A Brief History of Bridges & Tunnels

During the empty days that followed
the departure of the sirens
the woman walked along the dry corridor
of a long forgotten river

Picking her way through scarified remains
of cottonwoods and arroyo willows,
she followed the shadow of her former self,
itself a shadow

A plateau rose on the western bank
where the last of the great valley oaks
reached their mighty limbs towards
the hazy blue sky, conducting the final
movement for listening ghosts

Her shadow danced in the washed light
beneath the branches, upon the grasses;
she tread lightly, taking care to avoid
the ground-nesting wasps

She saw a faint impression of a road where,
from once-mute holes in the sun-baked earth,
an ancient sound issued forth –
the sound of humming

She put her ear to an old spider hole
and heard, echoing in the empty tunnel
between universes, a girl softly singing
Bury me not on the lone prairie

Whipped by the reins of a blind charioteer,
a band of a thousand racing thunderheads
blackened the sky, and the world wrested itself
from the prison of its form

Her shadow jumped headlong into the hole
leaving her standing there, shadowless;
she herself felt the heavy pull and swayed
but remained fixed, unmovable

Her grief was of a different matter, dark and exotic;
she stood strong as a taproot
against the flow of gravity's river
which emptied into who knows where

The vast landscape upheaved, moving towards
Spider Grandmother's hole in the hardpan –

the oaks, the cottonwoods and willows
the heat red rocks of a bone-dry river
the salmon carcasses and hubcaps
the ruminant skulls and beer cans
the fishing lines and mugworts
the farm shacks and rusted pumpjacks
the gypsum and shell hash
even the mighty dams, imperial and proud,
still hoarding their fetid puddles,
shook their very foundations while the
the terrible pumps spun backwards;
the highways began to flow
the windmills broke free and flew in

flocks like whirling white seabirds towards
the old spider hole
a space-time door in the floor,
to a highway of light through darkness

While the world disappeared
it was the woman's sad fate
to stay where the oak woodland
and the river and the mountains
where scrub jays, thrushes and warblers
where the possums and brush rabbits
were now not

Kneeling upon the emptying sands
she reached into the hole and felt
the warmth of a small hand,
pulled the girl to her feet and
saw, dimly, her long-forgotten self

Into the woman's hands, the girl
placed her own in one; in the other
for all that had been taken,
a single acorn was offered in return

*   *   *

In the absence of *things*
the absence of light was unnoticeable
and the woman understood
more clearly this time
that the touch of light upon
the objects of the world were
at once a brutal blow and gentle brush
and the story itself of a life

With the small hand in hers,
in trembling darkness, she asked the girl
which way was the way through

Walking, skipping, they stirred up tiny specks of
curious luminescent dust, which glowed
such as the lights she had seen in the sand
on a beach on a moonless night

Slowly the shape of a bridge
assembled itself before her straining eyes
but she could distinguish neither
end nor beginning, but only great depth
which she knew as the Chasm of Grief;
and she dared never look down
into the black abyss of unmaking

There, the molecules grieved
for having been part of a being
larger then themselves
a grief such as the fiddler feels
when the fire goes cold

Knowingly, the girl who was also herself
sang the song of small stars who,
in their lonely brilliance, long to dance
in the dappled sunlight of an autumn glade
and to sing:

Oh bury me not on the lone prairie
where the coyotes wail and the wind blows free—
And when I die don't bury me
beneath the Western sky on the lone prairie.

3. A Brief History of Roots

Across the Bridge of Voids
a blind and ancient woman
with high-knuckled hands
sat weaving in the blackness

With her Milky Way stare, the Weaver
wove the aerial roots of a strangler fig
as her mother and her grandmother
had done before her

The woman and the girl saw the
the snaking roots emerge from darkness
struggling towards a dim star only to be
waylaid at the Weaver's bridge

The old Weaver worked the roots
around the thin ruins of Time's tunnel
of which little more remained than
an invisible, vibrating string

A string the length of six miles
the width of one quivering note
less than a trillion times smaller
than the radius of a single hydrogen atom
yet heavy as the earth itself

Weaving is the work of all
who await the mother's return to where
the hills and valleys once resembled
the straw yellow hide of a lion

Where does the strangler fig grow?
asked the girl

The strangler figs grow here and there,
said the milky eyed Weaver, who sat
weaving the hanging bridges for eons

We too are like ancient trees who carry
with us, in our roots
in the clinging clumps of earth
memories of our native soil, persisting
though our homeland be lost
our hollowness unbearable

Like us, the roots recoil from their source
and lose themselves in desiring, grasping
within a dreaming Void,
while what we sought changes
past recognition while we sleep

The Weaver twisted a root,
supple and green, into a coil
then a hundred tiny tendrils sought
the smallest cracks in the great bridge
a space where they might insinuate themselves
into some brace of permanence

We are the Strangler Figs.
People have no respect for change
They despair of it.

And so, the woman learned certain things about roots:
such as not all roots are found in soil
some lay anchor to the host's limbs and trunk
fatally constricting vital layers

Some roots begin in the future and reach back
into the dry, scorched earth of the present
in search of nutrients and the clear water
for which they thirst

Some roots carry the blood of generations–
women, all of them Weavers –
whose tedious and tireless work
bridges all Great Chasms of Despair
across which, they pray, their mother
may one day return.

A Fauna of Mirrors

In ancient China some believed that
behind every mirror existed another world –
worlds inhabited by strange fauna
each adapted to its proper mirror
all unknown and strange to even
those men and women
who once knew the ways of
the Pig-footed Bandicoots
the Honsh Wolves
the Dusky Seaside Sparrows
the Golden Toads or
the rhinoceroses –
    the Blacks of the West and the Whites of the North.

Perhaps owing to industry
or a lack of imagination
the worlds behind the mirrors were shut
to us and our distrust of mirror worlds grew
as did the distorted portraits
in their reflections.

In the many thousands of years
since the worlds were shut
we have forgotten how to look
into these ancient mirrors -
those that shine in the end of an icicle
a quiet alpine lake
a chrome hubcap or a cup of coffee
the eye of a black snake
or a desert mirage.

We turned our attention instead
to those mirrors that spoke to us
and we believed we saw ourselves in them
as we truly are.

But beyond the quicksilvered surface
of all mirrors, infinite in number,
the Fauna yet lived in the myrtle forests,
sipping nectar from the yellow asphodel,
grazing in fields of cry pansy.

They hunted and slept
they drank from coldwater brooks
they burrowed, nested, and flapped
a million iridescent wings in the stirring breeze
while they called and mated, emerged and died.

They waded in the sheeting water
of a tide receding across the sugar fine sands
alight with streaks of fireball orange
scraping forth the evening sky.

> Borges took inventory of this fantastic menagerie.
> For all we know, may be among them now.

Only few mirrors remain
through which we may glimpse
the swaying of root-spine palms
or the canopy of Rhea's kapok tree
where the Lamed Wufniks
mourn their last sunrise as men.

And what of the cracked mirrors?
Somewhere on Earth, at midnight
a plastic hand mirror
perhaps dropped in the morning rush
harbors the last of the elusive black Ping Feng –
a pig with one proper head and another
where a tail should be.

Behind the persisting oil slick
gelatinous, clinging to the marsh grass
asphyxiating all life below
the slithering Hua Fish resides
foretelling drought to nobody listening.

In the coal black puddle that shivers
at the bottom of a mineshaft
the shy Quilin - famed unicorn of China
moves silently amidst the Wuda tree ferns
which once grew taller than an oak.

Quilin, protector of men
from the one-headed dog with two bodies
known as T'ao T'ieh the Ravenous,
longs to walk the overgrown roads,
the buckling tarmacs and fallen bridges
of our ancient cities.

One who might dare to look
into the poisoned slurry of the San Joaquin –
once a Tigres-Euphrates
now the Cocytus and Phlegethon

clutching at its parched throat —
One who might push aside the floating leaves
to strain away bad residues
may chance to glimpse the rare
rain bird — Shang Yang.

Shang Yang, by carrying river water
in her beak, brings the rains of winter
and could be of great comfort to us now.

Yet the Fauna of Mirrors
being of animal mind
has no memory of this place —
it does not remember the
well-traveled paths or viney doorways
between worlds.

It is said that the last time
anything bothered to come back
was to deliver us one of our own
— the Devourer of the Dead.

The Kermit Kingdom

Just yesterday I heard the expression
'Hermit Kingdom' for the first time
listening to a radio program about a
renegade celebrity on his way to
North Korea to stir the pot for a few
photo ops and some bad press.

I imagined first a kingdom
of hermits, each one alone in
a thatched roof house, nestled deep
in a primeval forest, or squalid muddy
hollows near an oyster shell beach
stinking of low tide and seaweed,
mumbling to their mice,
mourning their candle stubs.

I wondered – who would they
reign *over* if every subject
was so hermit-like, so troglodyte?

Then I wondered if I had in fact
heard it all wrong:
maybe what the host really said was
the 'Kermit Kingdom.'
I thought about it a while,
stuck in traffic at three p.m.
an American Imperialist
in my Japanese minivan.

The thought of it made me smile.

What a wonderful place this
could be - the Kermit Kingdom -
where the Royal Throne
is a mossy, fallen log
spanning a crooked brook
burbling and pristine.

This King holds court with a
little banjo on his knee,
empathizing sincerely
with his countrymen and women,
little tears falling from
the corners of his keyhole eyes,
about the universal
difficulties of being green.

In school every child writes songs
about rainbows without wondering why
there are so many and
as for what's on the other side, well
what we've been told is that
rainbows have nothing
to hide in Kermit's Kingdom.

The Queen is a pink pig in a feather boa—
the national icon of beauty and style;
some of the monsters love cookies

some have heads like a honeydew
some are beakers that sing 'Habanera'
but none are armed with
anything but arms for hugging.

Once in a while the Kermit King
loses his cool and flips out completely
but his friends – one of them a bear
one of them a shrimp
another a rat
one of them a gonzo –
set him right again in real time
there on live TV for all to see.

When the Kermit King addresses
his beloved people, we can
see the strings that make his mouth
and his arms move and yet,
unlike the puppets of the West,
unlike the puppets of the East,
we don't mind because
the truth is not hidden
from us, the viewers at home
and we love him all the more.

Like his fellow Emperors,
this Kermit King
has no clothes but was made

instead from a spring green coat
pilling from years of use
with two ping pong balls for eyes
made by a Patron Saint of children.

In Kermit's Kingdom
green is all there is to be.
It could make you wonder why,
but why wonder?

Pravda – a Found Poem

His skin, his blood was failing.
One had the same feeling as before:
the grim knowledge, two lives
unknown rivers flowing, two hearts.
Pieces, files, official papers
erupting from distant cabinets
rained down, aflame in a grim hour…

>Heavy fog on the Black Sea,
>Gas lights out in Moscow.

The other choice was to begin to notice –
the speeches, the press, propaganda,
to have always been struck, exhumed
by ironies of histories, its fatal incisions,
invoking God's help: Help us!
Such does the high wall of God surround
intolerable village republics.

More at the palace gates
than peasants crushed by a revolt;
more than soldiers marching though,
but specters uttering his name as
provocation when a party know-how
(one of the ringmasters –
a triumph-and-monument minister)
walked around and around the mad man.

>Far away.

They'd fired upon a few during a storm
shouts swallowed by the squall
men, aspirating bloody foam,
dark stain of hand-picked sailors
covering the lower deck.
Shipwrecks could receive
some last revolutionaries;
it had been arranged before.

These were ignored, laughed at
no hands left to help sort out
the tangles of a year of terror.

Expect none by sea – stop
Three assassinated in Moscow – stop
He's done breathing in a Kremlin apartment – stop.

They came when a bomb exploded
below a fretted archway.
They were nearby already, likely.

It's Serge, one said,
recording the remains,
blood on the broken marble,
witness to the confused stare of a child
forsaken in the shadowy doorway
still in her nightgown.

Cheer up! he said to small and motherless
Alexandra, and he sent a message
to the abbey when more small
causalities came forward.

I have been to Moscow and – stop
I have seen the Abbess – stop
She is of no ordinary vein
in her hooded habit
of pearly gray – stop
Oh, holy bosom of the motherland! – stop
She's got beds for all! – stop.

Lips like red blood droplets on fresh snow,
I am the hero of heroes.

He tugged at the abbey bell,
was angered when it clanged,
mocking ringing, haunting him
like the echoes of the rattling ship
where they'd thrown their
officers overboard.

He'd heard them whispering
in the Black Sea fog
the dead – dredged up, dragged back
on a dark passage, now wandering
ghosts at the palace gates.

It makes him sick to read about
one mad moment, one necessary misstep
in the paper - where is their *power*?

> The ministers assemble in the dark.
> They cackle without action.

Now an oldish man – an illiterate peasant
collects the pages of half-burned files
raining down upon his wheat fields
sailing in on crosswinds to this No Place,
another intolerable village republic.

Thoughtfully he puts pieces together
uniting war torn pages, lives.

In his life's winter yawn
he remembers a time when
many a young revolutionary
called himself a *soviet*.

He saves the papers of a comrade
celebrated in the Pravda,
all of them intact and stamped.
The dark haired boy in the photo
a sailor, or a spy perhaps
could be his own Alexi,
toiling, sweating in the fields,
who dreams always of Paris.

For #Camus on His 100th Birthday

    I.

Today, on Camus' 100th Birthday
230 million birds in the cloud
tweeting across the continents
signaling the coming of spring
with Arab spring still blooming
in a desert blackout
above the rising tide of revolution
amidst the emptying of holy lands.
Yet, the only question remaining
is still the question of suicide.

    II.

Back home the growers used this stuff
on the grass they grow in the redwoods.
Simply opening a single canister
of this illegal pesticide can kill you.

Today a Kansas school indefinitely
suspended a thirteen-year-old boy
for wearing a paisley purse.

Today, just north of my city
a young Latino
a child, your son or mine
gunned down by twitchy cops
on the streets of his city.
His city has no slides or swings;
his city is exposed by a violent sun

a city undone – our city.
Strange how this city I live in
becomes the city I'm from.

III.
Today, an Opportunity!
Visualizing a Time Challenge!
Live inside real-time –
the age of information
the emergent consciousness
of Remorseless Man.

IV.
How far back do Robots really go?
The singularity is so last year.
Hope was always the human error
they wished to avoid.

Time is an ugly, senseless horror
but they say Wal Mart brings work
like seeded clouds bring rain;
they say we should be grateful.

Robots help us fold laundry.
Today drones strike without warning.
Assembly line slaves don't have time
to conquer the world.

Pharaohs were the original Steampunks.
They had those crazy machines,
you know, they stored their souls
in jam jars.

V.
We wax poetic in the dark –
put yourself in my shoes.
Do remember those days?
Playing in the attic of the old house
after the sun went down
behind the live oak,
how we scanned the lines
of nine vintage books
about the afterlife of queers?

VI.
Hey friends, the Senate is voting right now!
Make some history!
Tweet it, post it, like it, tag it.

Read the signs of nuclear winter
in the cosmic tea leaves.
Speak to us in microtonal visions
special binary appearances
in the syntax and semantics
of modern hieroglyphics.

VII.
Binaural Beats, or
Why you can't sleep and what to do about it.

The lightning strikes our faces,
a blow from the fists of drunken fathers,
shadowboxing in the glassy darkness.

VIII.
In the beginning there was silence,
a silence neither poetic nor hermetic
but irredeemably desolate.
In retrospect we fought
the stubborn torpor without
a single moment of relief
in that epoch wherein our
infinite strangeness was suspended
in dust and spare parts.

IX.
Today. Finally, rain.

I just want to sit here,
to watch and listen.
It's been so long I almost forgot
how beautiful it can all be.

X.
The world is beautiful, and outside there is no salvation.

Eulogy for Sycorax

To the naive observer
she is an old fisherwoman, perhaps,
or a hovel dwelling hag.

Her coarse skirts hitched
above her sagging knees,
she wades alone at night
in the warm shallows
of the tropics under the blinking
bygone brilliance of a billion stars.

She might say to you,
stirring her witch's brew and
staring up at the Eternity machine,
that we have all been alive together, here
at this Fat Chance crossroads of space
in our drip-droplet of Time
a blip from bang to wheeze
in which all histories become one
in Gravity's dying breath.

Upon the Dog Star
she may make a last wish:
to stand at the water's edge and
to hold, once more, the warm hand
of her only son snugly in her own,
to catch the scent of coconut
and Castile soap
in the tangled copper curls
of her island cherub.

Never did there live
such a man
as Caliban.

She hauls in poles of far away trees
felled in distant storms
arriving on the tide
with a thousand green bottles
cork bobbing in the whitewash
bearing such desperate messages
from so many lonely places.

She steps across the stinking mounds of
starfish, spent by some plague
of the waves sent by Proteus.

She makes no guesses as to when
the primary dreamer
of this world will awaken from
her prolonged paralysis, asleep
in the sealed up chambers
of those sublime organelles –
the mind palace of Progress:

>   buildings with no windows
>   schools with no yards
>   dams with no rivers
>   empty ports and stations
>   prairies shrinking below the
>   asphalt wonders of the world.

She may wish, as the hour draws near,
to know our Time for what it is:
the story we tell ourselves
to lighten the leaden grief
wrought in the final moments
when our atoms abandon us
but mourn us nonetheless.

When at last her eyes fail,
she begins to see the patterns
in all things, above and below,
from the tiniest roots
to the frailest twigs
winter sleeping
bud-dreaming of bees
and the sweet perfume of her garden
where the Ilex Oak grows
anchored in the bedrock of the
ancient rivalries between
space and solidness
into and out of which
all spirits pass freely.

In this solemn moment
wherein she witnesses the
blazing bauble of the sun extinguish
in the darkening sea – a sea
rocked and angered by the
hostility of storms and hurricanes,
soothed by the lapping tide –
a free child of low birth

scavenges bobbing fruit
in the warm and saline waters
chasing gulls down the wide beach
constructing palaces
of driftwood and kelp
watching the wading shorebirds
make the first marks of writing
in the island sands
as they did then
and do now.

Our Sycorax is a liquid state –
a creature of neither house
nor mountain but a great energy
of the valleys and great basins
the sinks of the oceans
calderas and gypsum caves
of storm clouds racing across the sea.

She gives little thought to scribes
at the moment she joins with
ever changing waters
swimming in the deep
Protean domain,
waiting to be reborn.

Half Savage and Free

They'd sought no probable explanation
no disambiguation of class,
(order, family, genus)
for the idiot in the courtyard,
filing his nails with flint,
painting the stone walls
with his own excrement.

A few had teased her for
a nose, an eye, a grimace
a shadow of the Hapsburg jaw
perceived in the child.
But for a red-faced cousin
(rapacious brute with a lazy eye)
lurking by the dolly tubs after dark,
the truth was known to none
but Kate.

These days, one does not know
Queen Victoria from Miss Ape.
By the burning brambles certainly
there were water carriers – slaves
inured to far-off mutterings,
to the rustling grasses
and drifting sands –
to the birds.

You know, some scholars
would bet their sunny reputations
that Moses was high.

This feeling of foolishness
inside the echo chambers of
Royals that talk too much
if only say that Helena
was a hemophiliac
like her grandmother
(though it was little talked about)
and then with Charles D. who claims
to have seen things in a new light
attaching less importance to
divine intervention, design.

After a few years of bumping
around the Galapagos then
puttering about in his little garden,
granting agency to all things equally
(turtles, finches, white rabbits)
he made a mockery of the old lines.
Such are the hazards of Royals –
fecund, rich, spoiled.

They'll have us marrying
scullery maids and smithies
before long!

And what to make of these hemophiliacs bloodlines?

Kate was the first to
fall ill with pneumonia;
an entire line, all in one house,
gone in a single winter's night
except for the colicky infant
fast asleep in the cradle
of the wet nurse's arms.

In the morning, to let the air in,
a maid, barely seventeen,
pulls back the heavy curtains
that exhale their consumptive dust
into the emptied rooms of the great house
something veiled and creeping
inside these echo chambers.

She waves to the smithy's son
passing through the gate
with a posy of fresh violets
in his breast pocket.

The innocent orphan turns
towards the window.
Heir to a Godless dynasty,
with none to sprinkle the dirty
water of the parish font upon her,
she may yet take root
in this sunless world.

The Expedition

After passing more gas giants
than he could count,
after stalling for days
at a failed brown dwarf,
a small, fastidious archeologist
from the exo-planet Tau Boötis Ab
landed on a smaller, bluer planet
that had been emitting faint
biological signatures
on its journey around
a tired star.

Curatorial by nature,
he searched for relics
with his magnetic relic sensors;
he did not find:

>ceramic shards,
>a jaw bone or a
>skull with an axe wound,
>ceremonial attire
>temples buried by the sands of time
>broken by vines and lichens
>a dormant seed –
>nothing from the
>holographic archives
>of past digs.

Instead, at the bottom of a barren plain,
he found a small sticky label,
stuck to a piece of hide, or
to the rind of something
mostly made of carbon
black and mummified and
possibly preserved by
adhesives from a tiny tag
bearing the faded glyphs
'84033 O-R-A-N-G-E.'

He found no other biologics anywhere.
His life-form detecting scanner
went silent on the subject.

He checked his map
then scratched the little
silica strands on his bulbous
translucent skull where two halves
of his brains rose and sank
like blobs of molten wax in a lava lamp.

The archaeologist,
fastidious and thorough,
cursed with tedious longevity,
spent the best light years
of his life searching impact craters
volcanic vents, suspect alluvium,
vast seabeds, long since evaporated
by a cataclysm the great makers
of the mystical sticky dot
didn't see coming.

He analyzed every molecule
in the cylindrical sections
taken by the advanced
core drills of his tiny probe
until at last he packed up his calipers
his sieves and brushes
his trowels and scales
his pegs, pins and nails
tools he remade in the likeness
of those used by ancient giants
in his field.

Believing his reputation in ruins
and that he would return
his native Tau Boötis Ab.
with nothing but a hard luck story,
he caught the wormhole home
sleeping much of the way.

He awoke with sharp pains in his head
and a groggy epiphany.
He reversed engineered the specimen
and grew out an orange, a frog,
a singing mouse, a scorpion
and a deadly virus.

The fastidious archaeologist paced
the tunnels of his laboratory
until the singing mouse
sang him a sad story – an epic tale of
of missed chances and gross oversight.

Today, in the great city of Tau Boötis Ab
pilgrims visit the great pyramid,
taller than the tallest building
made of pure, crystalline carbon
that is rumored to contain
within its impenetrable walls,
under guard for eternity,
a deadly relic, organic in origin,
with a sticky label –
a warning to all.

The Strait of Messina

Summon the selkies, the freshwater fishes
Shuck the black oysters in sea wormwood dishes
Let the Sea King dream as the shearwaters scream
Ten bits in the pot for your wasted last wishes.

> *The luminous wind-gall is the least of her charms*
> *But when she starts blowing great guns and small arms*
> *Any port in a storm will do, merry men,*
> *Any port in a storm will do.*

Bring cards and a bottle to succor thy souls
Sail silently under the black Sacks of Coals
Whisper the waters - *the Scylla awaits*
We make for the ballow to slip past the shoals.

> *Boldering weather is the least of her charms*
> *But when she starts blowing great guns and small arms*
> *Any port in a storm will do, merry men,*
> *Any port in a storm will do.*

Turn not to the blunderbuss, saker and cannon
Rum up the tongue to lively the Chanty Man
Offer Charybdis your Abraham-men
Incidit in scyllam cupiens vitare charybdim.

> *Blusterous bunk is the least of her charms*
> *But when she starts blowing great guns and small arms*

Any port in a storm will do, merry men,
Any port in a storm will do.

Keep her rap-full! See the cavernous maw!
The great horned claw, the spikey toothed jaw
A debt we must pay for our bird catching days
See the pull-away-boys row swiftly away
Charybdis, old girl, she'll swallow us raw!

Ready About! The storm petrels swarm
She's already blowing great guns and small arms
Yea, any port in a storm would have done, merry men
Any port in a storm would have done!

The Visitors

I always know when my neighbor
sits down to compose a few lines
by the arrival of a young woman
with a peachy complexion
a dusting of freckles across her cheeks
on her head, a wreath of freesia and satin ribbons.

You can't help but notice her youthful bloom,
how she bursts from her peasant smock,
how the sultry breeze lifts
the flowing train of her hair
catching the sunlight
in flags of molten copper.

Dancing down the walkway
in hemp skirts and shoeless feet
with dime store bells about her ankles,
she brings jars of raw honey and,
for reasons unclear to me then,
three ducklings in a willow basket.

My mother's heavy drapes
exhale a long-held breath
from folds of their black lungs.
Choking on the foul vapors of exhumation
on powdery clouds of mildew and dust.
I spy his bald pate from my
upstairs window, watching
as he scurries into the house,

locking all the doors as he so
delights in her *sneaking* in.

Through the branches
of an ancient and dour cypress,
head mistress of my shady yard,
I strain to see this Thalia
fertile, bounding, laughing,
as she climbs through
the window of his kitchen
leaving a flurry of crab apple petals
hanging in the heavy air
before she vanishes inside.

And so I know his wife
is away on the dull errands
that a marriage to a man
of his many talents demands.

His muse sets his books in order
She fills the jars with ice and lemon water
licking the honeyed spoon.
She reserves two box seats
to see the Chinese acrobats then
sews herself a silk dress,
of fire engine red, hand embroidered
with abalone buttons.

She reads to fill his head with
age old teachings of the sages,
of the bards and sorcerers

of the cave dwelling magi
of the hermits and ecstatics
of young lovers and wise women.

She scrubs and polishes and
feeds him buttered bread.
In her pond-water eyes she
earns the favor of gods both
wrathful and lascivious.

By skill or by witchcraft,
the lucid dreams of men
    – of the poets and the Troubadours
    – of the priests and rabbis
    – of common park bench creeps
dreams in which they trace
the soft, pink flesh of her breasts
the gentle curve of her waist
with their groping eyes,
their bony fingers
are awakened in him.

As sure as eggs is eggs, my neighbor is
rewarded with much success
and widespread admiration.

After five weeks of rain
when the black mold advances
across the kitchen ceiling,
when the years of tiny, pattering feet
of warm and dimpled hands

and strawberry kisses have past,
when the pipes are leaking
and the wires have all gone bad
when the foundation rots in the ground
and Byron's darkness falls in
a lump of death – a chaos of hard clay,
it is only then I hear the familiar
knock of wretched knuckles on my door
the knock of desperation.

My old friend Achlys – the muse of gloom,
shrouded in the mist of wintry fields
arrives in an aromatic cloud of ferment and moth balls.

Pale, bone thin, and weeping
with chattering teeth, swollen knees,
crescents of black dirt below her long nails
her cheeks scratched and bloodied,
her shoulders covered with thick
pollen from the crab apple blossoms,
she scrapes her muddy boots
upon my threadbare rug,
shakes the rain from rag mop hair,
upon the only pages
I've managed to complete.

The ink runs black
in little rivulets over the paper,
the desk, and onto the floor.
She tells me, in a solemn voice
that there is no point in writing

anything else; she proceeds
to list the host of coming plagues
that promise to eliminate life
as we know it, and in just a few
generations too, and how the West
is to blame for everything
with their appetites for gadgets,
for speed and strange salads.

But then the little stream of water
pools upon the floor in a moonscape
of inky pots so we stare a while.

When the sun breaks through
the clouds – orange, pink and white
reflected new in shimmering puddles –
molten drops of gold upon the wood
of the kitchen floor –
an oil sheen, then a nebula
rotating in the cosmic stew.

We watch the changes.
We go way back, me and my Achlys.

In a while, she wonders out loud
what new metaphor
could ever arise from spilled ink
seeping through the floorboards –
now only a stain upon a memory.

What a clatter and racket!
Such screams of delight as
Thalia pushes down the fence!

Spry and sure-footed as a cow,
she crashes through my yard,
my neighbor's livid wife snipping
madly at her hair, brandishing
her beloved pruning shears
until Thalia, not looking,
collides with the great trunk
of the old cypress in my backyard
spilling words in every language
she'd hidden in the shredded paper –
bedding for the ducklings
in her basket of gifts.

Kabocha

Green, warty and humble,
this small Japanese cousin
of the buttercup squash
has a cult following among
pumpkin enthusiasts.

Known for its mango flesh
its smooth texture, its chesnutty flavor,
the kabocha is revered as an aphrodisiac
by squashophilic peoples of the globe.

If you have a large enough knife
to cleave this rock-hard squash-bauble,
the fragrance from its secret chamber
will make you believe in fairy godmothers.

The scent is recognizable
to anyone who has dug their bare hands
into the soil beneath the late-winter leaf mould
– fermented, pungent, cool
ripe with humus, alive with springtails.

For most, any amorous feelings that arise
from eating the kabocha
are directed towards the human heart
and not the pumpkin itself, as in my case.

I often bake the kabocha whole
to avoid the problem of breaking its hull;

I have been plunged, on occasion
into aromatic confusion
as the baking fills the kitchen with the scent –
I kid you not – of a sweating horse.

To any girl who has lived through
obsession with the *Equus caballus*
the plastic models, show ribbons,
the complete *Misty of Chincoteague* collection
(although Misty was technically a pony),
to her, sweating horse is the smell of Freedom.

Speaking of which, Sham –
the steed of my childhood,
my foul-tempered Rosinante
whose passion for running me
under low branches resulted
in at least two hairline fractures,
a few swollen ticks in the thigh,
and ten or so stitches.

Sham spent his golden years
grazing on a hill behind my house
on Montford – a place known
to all the feral children of Homestead
abandoned, as we were, in the weedy summers
to wander the bramble-choked deer trails
that traversed the mountain.

We hunted for blue-green liquor bottles
in the Eucalyptus grove by the old farmhouse

where the tenants – communal in numbers,
dancing naked on the deck
smoking their hookah pipes
and their hand rolled joints –
let us scamper, run wild like vermin.

Only years later did I learn Kerouac
had written *Dharma Bums* within
those very walls – hung with saris and sarongs
reeking with patchouli and ginger beer.

With a power unmatched by color
the baking kabocha reclaims the dreamer,
leading her by the ankle bangles, dancing
in a free-association revelry, lucid tripping
through the perfumed labyrinths of memory.

In the year of Sham came *Polyester*
out in Odoroma – better than 3-D by far.
I saved my Scratch 'N Sniff cards for years
on behalf of all persecuted heroines
Divine, or otherwise.

In the chemical signatures of Odorama –
burning flesh, dog shit and new car,
my memory traced a line
from the purple vinyl couches
the red velvet cushions in the Castro Theater,
the clouds of carbon dioxide
coughed out by my father's Camaro,
Etzel shouting down the dumbwaiter

at Sam Wo's and the grease of Chow Fun,
to the face of Dexter the foot-fetishist
and his kindred spirit in life,
the faceless trail-side killer of Mt. Tam.

One day a farmer will grow a
Kabocha big enough to hide away in –
Cinderella's carriage
in a world without clocks
and ill-fitting slippers of glass
where the walls are edible,
the doorways hung with
with seed-strung curtains.

I will ride upon the top, madly whipping
the reins, the wind groping at my hair
with its icy claws, while
all the silent watchers in the forest spy
from the haunted hollows of black night
as the old horse draws me swiftly
away to a truer freedom
than the Dharma Bums
could ever grant a Cinderella.

For I, too, *would rather sit on a pumpkin,*
and have it all to myself
than be crowded on a velvet cushion.

For Wendy

Sagacious peach!
Sturdy in her mud-caked boots,
her white hair - a dandelion mane.

She walks, alive with the riotous laughter
of water running over stones
speaking with the wisest of the
old willows that grow along
the banks of Redwood Creek.

Oh! Patron Saint of Nettles
champion of the lowly springtail,
keeper of the soil's dark secrets,
we beg her - do not leave us to suffer
in a world of watery tomatoes!

Instead, across an abyss of time and state lines,
she invites forth the Seneca Nation –
guardians of the Western Door.

Though wary of our West Coast ways,
they teach us the wisdom
of the Three Sisters:
we learn that to save the bear bean
the squash and gourds,
the Iroquois corn,
is to save ourselves.

As we look uncertainly at one another
in the dappled plains of understory
we are invited to dance
beneath the coast live oak
with the Hamadryads,
losing ourselves in the absurdity
of old limbs and stiff backs,
rolling our ankles on acorns.

In the borrowed words of Alan Chadwick
Wendy tells us, her unruly students –
The garden makes the gardener;
the farm makes the farmer.

And we whisper back –
And so patience makes the teacher.

Open Letter to Mammon

A muddy touché to you, Mammon
and your company of thieves –
robber barons of Hong Kong and Dubai,
fork-tongued brothers of the bible belt!

We applaud the handing over
of our stolen goods.

May we offer you a free-of-charge
gondola ride over the Holy Land,
a bird's-eye view of your assets –
your mothers and daughters, your brides
your pimps, your priests and pederasts
your arms traders and factory generals
your Legacy on its death march –
advancing with the Exodus
in the shadow of a thunderhead
towards absolution in a wine dark sea.

Desiccated by desert heat
the old, the weak, and the very young
and those beyond utility
shall remain eternally entombed
in the vaults of the sun.

Some are set adrift, wandering
the empty streets and alleys
where the Etesian flutes
echo through the columns

of lonely island temples.
Still others, inhabitants of bygone ice
of the high steppes and atolls,
of the Dengue jungles,
of the sand spit nations –
by your leave they join the fate of those
dragging their feet from Bethlehem
with the taste of Dead Sea salt
on their blue-black tongues.

Yet you, Mammon, high and haughty
your abacus and deeds at hand,
spitting crimson betel juice
on the shoeshine boy
from the City of God,
on the shoeshine girl
from the City of Angels,
grinning, your grill glinting
as the laborers of your camps
vacate the bloated bowels
of your Mega Babylons
of your creeping outskirts
of your suburban Irkallas
with their rent-a-Nergals
festering like a thousand poxes
upon the continents.

Forgetting, they abandon the stragglers
shake breadcrumbs from their pockets
toss silver coins to the trade rats
over their skinny shoulders.

Mammon, do you remember
your little chochita with
pinto bean skin?
She hides poison darts
under her Shakira beach towel
and she is coming for you first, hombre.

Yesterday, a reactor meltdown in Japan,
Tomorrow the monarch perishes
in a rain of highway shoulder poisons,
meanwhile the microbeads assemble in
near shore waters;
they are watching you like
a billion billion billion
primitive eyes in the waves.

Mammon, blind devil that you are,
in your palace of moth and rust
there will be none left
to know what the polecat ate,
no one to hear the gasping
of the Vaquita and Silky Sifafka
of the Mekong Catfish
as they sink below the surface of
the rising seas.

> The widening gyre spins in
> a kaleidoscope
> of shampoo bottles.
>
> Throw a rock through
> the liquor store window –
> Go to Jail dot com.

You and your black market organ traders
who sleep like infants and fear nothing
if not the loss of your Legacy –
you must know that It too will be buried
in the sub-sea archives.

Your last wishes will be recorded
in the annals of the lithosphere
lost in the subduction zones
guarded by tube worms –
great scholars of the deep.

Mylar Sirens

I

She is fast asleep
in a nest of black feathers –
Raven, black creator of worlds,
still oaring over the highway,
when a seagull wakes her.

A pitiless sun shines its
pitiless light upon
the hotel windows
reflecting a blank
and glaring gaze
towards the sea.
The sky – a whirl of gulls.
Here is a seaside city
she has never seen.

Is this in a book she wonders.
Is this the Fin de Siècle?
Women in sun hats stroll along the boardwalk.
A trolley rumbles past the arcade.

   She's got electric boots, a mohair suit

She stumbles blindly
in the ice blink
from one room to the next,
from one dark dream
to another, suspecting
she might still be asleep.

From the passenger windows
of her memory, houses from
different neighborhoods
cities, epochs, stories,
race by out there, outside
the trembling glass.

The face of a man, a ghost
(she can barely make it out)
materializes, quivering
in the pastel blur of
row houses rushing by.
If she could slow the picture
down she might hear what
he is saying.

At the end of the line
she recalls vaguely a stench,
a fetid inlet below the tracks
on the bridge stinking of creosote
where the sewage pipe
vomits the gray-brown bile
of the city's stomach
through its rusted mouth.

Time drains towards the sea.
A heron drops by to fish in
the scum-choked reeds.

> *The spotlight's hitting something*
> *that's been known to change the weather*

She recalls vaguely
the Mylar balloon in the algal froth,
the wrinkled words *Congratulations!*
sucking into metallic folds.

The Raven with
tattered wings cries
on the electric wire where
sneakers hang in a dead man's drop
above the drainage pipe –
spittoon of the city.

Plastic, taffy-colored
lids bob in the scum among
soggy dry cleaning coupons.
A battered transistor radio
transmitting a last sermon –
threats of an angry god
from a static dimension.

She recalls a blinding sun
mirage-making on asphalt rivers
casting stark shadows
against the concrete canal wall,
shadows of wasted things –
a grocery cart with two wheels
a piece of chain link fence
an orange highway cone
Ban de Soleil for a Central Bay Tan bottles
a maggoty, sodden doll
a heron with its wing spread
across a figure in the rushes.

When she and her sister were young,
they made a puppet theater
from a washing machine box.
A bare light bulb lit the stage
casting eerie flat shadows
from the hand puppets against
the pastel sky and the sea
she'd painted with tempura
on a white mailing envelope
for their flat world.

She tells figure in the dead man's float:
Time stops in the confluence of stagnant waters.

>   *We shall survive, let us take ourselves along*
>   *where we fight our parents out in the streets*

Memory festers in the mud puddles
of yesterday's floods and yet,
where currents now move, the
last pages of a diary
are drawn under and resurface;
its many worlds dissolve and disperse.

II

She is six now.
It might be summer on the Atlantic shore –
no pelicans flying over the sands
at this gloomy seaside resort.

She sits at a glass table
with a box of crayons
coloring leprechauns green,
clover and pots of gold.
In a high-rise apartment
she's got an eagle's nest view
of a flat, gray sea.

Two women in floral pantsuits
(one might be her mother)
sit upon an ochre couch,
talking, smoking, eating Chex Mix,
flicking ashes in the heavy
crystal ashtray set next to a
glass figurine of a terrier,
a box of matches from the Oyster Shack.

One – perhaps her mother –
picks at the gold threads
of a needlepoint pillow:
two nudes at a beach.
The other woman has
skin like Spanish leather.

She wears coral lipstick,
she is a bouquet of Pine Sol,
peppermint and tobacco.

At the end of a windowless hallway
they wait for the elevator.
Twenty floors down, down, down
to the small, gray pool, gape mouthed –
a hungry drain at the bottom of the world
below the tower which the girls thinks
is more like a machine.

Not a patch of dappled light here
to soften the grassy expanses
between the shoreline palms.
The two women smoke and gossip
by the pool while the girl's eyes
burn with chlorine and salt.

Across the highway is a beach,
long and featureless.
The gray water churns
under cloud darkened skies.
Something slips below the surface.

She thinks:
The world is flat and featureless.
The pool is the gaping mouth of a concrete earth.

She listens:
Someone is getting divorced.
Someone took pills and died.

There is insurance and paperwork.
I never should have had children - my figure!
A pilot crashed at the airshow
with everyone watching. On the Gulf.
It might have been a suicide.

The row houses rush by.
She is seven now.

Her father is drunk as a sailor.
The officers have gone home.
The rent is late.
Cockroaches are the size of your hand in these parts.
Bennie and the Jets skips on the turntable.
The beating is for scratching the record.
It's okay for kids to get high, says her father.
We all gotta die sometime.

   Man, I'm so spaced out.

Blue sky, the skirmish of clouds.
The wheels spark on the tracks.

She is ten now.
The light has gone out of her sister's eyes,
or was put out – she's not sure.
They sit on the kitchen floor
waiting for the hamster, escaped again,
to peep out of a hole.
They are hungry as thieves.
The roof rats run.

Their mother sleeps all day.
Nothing in the kitchen
but sugar and salt to eat.

The sand on the Gulf was as white as sugar,
says her sister. *Yes,* says the girl.
But you were too young to remember.

B-b-b-b-bennie and the jehehehehets.

She dreams her mouth is full of sand.
Some kids can't hold their breath.
She hates the word *roach*.

> When she was a little girl
> with little golden curls,
> there once was a man
> who had a white van.
>
> The van had no windows
> The van had no doors,
> Just seagrass shag carpet
> and bones on the floor.
>
> She found some bee bees
> when she was down on her knees.
> The man with the van says:

So stick around
You're gonna hear electric music
Solid walls of sound!

The smoking woman in the pantsuit
who lives in the towers
with the pool like a gaping hole
at the bottom of the world
says ugly little girls tell lies.

Once the girl dreamed the drain
in the bathtub sucked her down.

She swam through the other side
holding her breath until
she reached the surface
of the reservoir where
hundreds of swept away children
swam close to the earthen dam,
swam with their eyes shut
in the cold gray water
in the featureless dirt land.
None of them drowned.

III

She is back at the inlet
stagnant, stinking below
the tracks. No, the canal.
A figure in footed pajamas
bobs face down in the rushes.

How will her sister know to look for her here?
Her eyes went dim years ago.

> *Hey kid, shake it loose together*, says the heron.
> *The spotlight's hitting something –*

Spreading a wing to shade her
From the tractor beam sun
in the city of angels,
the heron tells her to *Let go!*
She begins to drift in the algal froth.

The sirens sing:
 Oh but they're weird and they're wonderful.

She floats on an inching current in the canal –
water that drips towards sea.

 She plugs into the faithless.

Her sister's voice whispers in the shallows.
 If you tell them, they will put your lights out.
 Now is the age of gentler things, the girl says.

She is so far from home
here on the floor of the sea
where the drift-mud sinks and settles.

A Spanish galleon glides on the surface.
The sun is cosmic nimbus
behind the pillow-white sails that billow,
darkening the sky in shifting eclipses.

She makes out the friezing –
a wooden siren with eyes wide open.
From the ship's deck
the trill of a deckhand's fiddle
fills her limbs with life.

A fiddle crab scurries
across a fishtail unfolding
where she once had legs.
She'd dreamt so long of the sea.

Here the seagrass, sways in the gentle surf
below the green waters.
She drifts among her many sisters,
drowned with their long hair swaying
like lullabies in the seagrass beds.

Their eyes are closed, their lips smile.
There is music and they rise, one by one
to join the chorus in the quaking forests
of brown kelp.

Each makes a dark silhouette
against the liquid sky as they swim
spiraling, spinning upwards
through the cool green fathoms.

She will join the sirens in their song
of all lost sisters who once lived
at the speed of light
among savages.

www.ingramcontent.com/pod-product-compliance
Lightning Source LLC
Chambersburg PA
CBHW020902020526
44112CB00052B/1204